MOM'S
—— LIFE JOURNAL ——

STORIES, MEMORIES AND MOMENTS
FOR MY FAMILY

The Life
Graduate
PUBLISHING GROUP

A LIFETIME OF LEARNING.

With over 100 titles ranging from self-help books, journals, diaries, personalised gift books, sporting journals and educational resources, we have a book for everyone!

CONTENTS

MOM'S
LIFE JOURNAL

MOM'S
LIFE JOURNAL

INTRODUCTION

Every parent has a story to tell, although many are never provided with the opportunity to share or capture those special memories, moments and stories in one place.

This journal has been carefully designed so parents can share their life story and provide the answers to many questions that family and friends have never asked.

· ·

Mom, use this journal to share your life experiences and your stories, memories and moments will remain a forever keepsake for generations to come.

Thank you for sharing your life story.

MOM'S INTRODUCTION

A Message From Mom

Mom's Introduction

A message before I begin.

_____

_____

_____

_____

_____

_____

_____

_____

_____

_____

_____

_____

_____

FULL NAME   DATE

Family Tree

Great-Grandmother

Great-Grandmother

Great-Grandfather

Great-Grandfather

Grandmother

Grandfather

Mother

Me

Great-Grandmother

Great-Grandmother

Great-Grandfather

Great-Grandfather

Grandmother

Grandfather

Father

My Sibling

My Sibling

My Sibling

My Sibling

My Sibling

My Sibling

SECTION ONE
THE BEGINNING

MY BABY YEARS

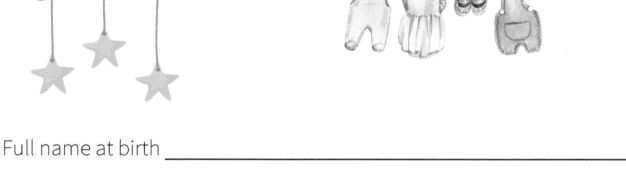

Full name at birth _____

Date of birth _____

Home address when born? _____

_____

Mother's name_____

Father's name_____

_____

The background to my birth name.

_____

_____

_____

MY LIFE JOURNAL

My father's age when I was born_____

Nationality_____

My father's occupation_____

My mother's age when I was born_____

Nationality_____

My mother's occupation_____

Names and ages of my siblings (if applicable)

_____

_____

_____

Were you in good health as a baby?

_____

_____

_____

Names of uncles and/or aunt's when you were born (as applicable)

_____

_____

_____

MY LIFE JOURNAL

Share with us some information about your parents.

_____

_____

_____

_____

_____

_____

_____

_____

_____

Grandparent Details

Mothers side.

Grandmother _____ Nationality _____

Grandfather _____ Nationality _____

Fathers side

Grandmother _____ Nationality _____

Grandfather _____ Nationality _____

This is something that you may not know about our family history.

_____

_____

_____

_____

_____

_____

_____

_____

_____

_____

_____

_____

_____

_____

_____

_____

MY LIFE JOURNAL

Use these pages to include any photos or further information about your family or baby years.

SECTION TWO
GROWING UP

MY CHILDHOOD YEARS

What is your earliest memory as a child?

_____

_____

_____

_____

_____

Were you told of any funny things or unique characteristics you had as a toddler?

_____

_____

_____

_____

_____

_____

_____

MY LIFE JOURNAL

As a toddler, what games or activities did you like to play?

_____

_____

_____

_____

_____

What was your favourite toy growing up?

_____

_____

_____

_____

Did you have a pet or any pets as a young child?

_____

_____

_____

_____

_____

MY LIFE JOURNAL

Did you have a favourite television show you loved to watch as a child?

_____

_____

_____

_____

What was your favourite book or books that you loved as child?

_____

_____

_____

Do you recall being involved in any accidents or hurting yourself as a young child? If so, is there a story behind the accident or injury?

_____

_____

_____

_____

_____

_____

_____

_____

MY LIFE JOURNAL

Was there a moment you recall getting into big trouble as a child? Was there a punishment?

_____

_____

_____

_____

_____

_____

_____

Was there a special celebration that you recall attending as a child?

_____

_____

_____

_____

_____

_____

MY LIFE JOURNAL

What are your fondest memories between the ages of 5 - 12?

_____

_____

_____

_____

_____

_____

_____

_____

_____

_____

_____

_____

_____

_____

_____

_____

MY LIFE JOURNAL

Use these pages to include any childhood photos.

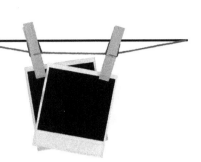

MY LIFE JOURNAL

What was your favourite meal as a child?

_____

Did you have any close friends as a child? If so, please provide some names and details.

_____

_____

_____

_____

_____

_____

Was there a sport or special interest that you started participating in at a young age?

_____

_____

_____

_____

_____

EARLY SCHOOL YEARS

My elementary/primary school was called...

_____

Provide the school location details.

_____

Describe your school. Was it in a city or rural location? Was it large or small? What were some of the backgrounds of the children that attended?

_____

_____

_____

_____

_____

_____

_____

_____

MY LIFE JOURNAL

Was there a teacher that really stood out to you that made an impact on your childhood or education?

_____

_____

_____

_____

Provide details of your most memorable moment or story from your early school years.

_____

_____

_____

_____

_____

_____

_____

_____

_____

MY LIFE JOURNAL

Did you have any close friends at school?

_____

_____

_____

_____

What kind of student were you? Were you well-behaved or mischievous?

_____

_____

_____

_____

_____

_____

_____

_____

_____

MY LIFE JOURNAL

What were your favourite subjects?

_____

_____

_____

Was there anything that you found challenging or difficult during your early school years?

_____

_____

_____

_____

_____

_____

_____

_____

_____

_____

MY LIFE JOURNAL

Use these pages to include any photos or further notes from your early school years.

MY TEENAGE YEARS

Describe what you were like as a teenager.

_____

_____

_____

_____

_____

_____

_____

What were your key interests?

_____

_____

_____

_____

_____

Did you date anyone in your teenage years? If so, share some details or a story.

Is there anything you regret doing as a teenager?

When and where did you learn to drive a vehicle?

_____

_____

_____

At what age did you get your vehicle licence? _____

What was your first vehicle/mode of transport that you purchased?

_____

_____

Share an experience from your early years of driving.

_____

_____

_____

_____

_____

_____

_____

_____

MY LIFE JOURNAL

Use this page to include a photo of a vehicle you have owned.

MY LIFE JOURNAL

Was there a particular kind of music that you enjoyed listening to in your teens?

_____

_____

_____

What was a favourite movie from your teens?

_____

_____

_____

What were some of the hobbies or activities that you enjoyed most as a teenager?

_____

_____

_____

_____

_____

_____

_____

MY LIFE JOURNAL

Was there a special holiday destination that you visited? If so, provide some details.

_____

_____

_____

_____

_____

_____

_____

_____

_____

_____

List 3 words that best describe you as a teenager?

1. _____

2. _____

3. _____

Did you attend High School? If so, where was it located and what was it called?

_____

_____

_____

What subjects did you enjoy at High School?

_____

_____

_____

Did you have a close friendship group? If so, provide some names and details.

_____

_____

_____

_____

_____

_____

_____

_____

MY LIFE JOURNAL

Describe one of your most memorable accomplishments at school.

_____

_____

_____

Did you have a nickname at school?

_____

_____

With what you know now, would you have done anything differently as a teenager?

_____

_____

_____

_____

_____

_____

_____

Use this page to include any High School photos or extra details.

MY LIFE JOURNAL

Do you have any other stories, memories or moments from your teenage years that you would like to share?

SECTION THREE

WHEN I WAS..

MY LIFE JOURNAL

When I was a child, I always looked forward to....

_____

_____

_____

When I was a teenager, I always dreamed of becoming...

_____

_____

_____

When I was a teenager, the biggest news story I can recall was...

_____

_____

_____

When I was growing up, my three favourite movies were...

1. _____

2. _____

3. _____

MY LIFE JOURNAL

When I completed school, the year was... _____

When I turned 21 yrs, I celebrated by....

_____

_____

_____

When I was in my teens, the silliest thing I did was.....

_____

_____

_____

When I was in my teens, I had a celebrity crush on....

_____

_____

When I was growing up, my three favourite bands were..

1. _____

2. _____

3. _____

MY LIFE JOURNAL

When I was young, I regret not...

_____

_____

_____

_____

_____

When I was a teenager, I earned some money by....

_____

_____

_____

_____

_____

When I left home for the first time, I went and lived....

_____

_____

_____

_____

_____

MY LIFE JOURNAL

These are the lessons I learnt as a teenager that I wish to pass onto my children and grandchildren.

_____

_____

_____

_____

_____

_____

_____

_____

_____

_____

_____

_____

_____

_____

_____

_____

SECTION FOUR
PARENTHOOD

MY LIFE JOURNAL

BECOMING A PARENT

My age when I first became a parent _____

Where were you living when you became a first time parent?

_____

_____

Explain how you felt emotionally when you became a parent?

_____

_____

_____

_____

_____

_____

_____

Was there anything that you were under-prepared for?

_____

_____

_____

_____

MY LIFE JOURNAL

My employment when I had my first child.

_____

_____

_____

If you have other children, list the locations and dates they were born.

Name	Location	D.O.B
_____	_____	_____
_____	_____	_____
_____	_____	_____
_____	_____	_____
_____	_____	_____
_____	_____	_____

How many children had you planned to have?

_____

_____

_____

MY LIFE JOURNAL

Use these pages to include some parenting photos

What has been your biggest challenge as a parent?

_____

_____

_____

_____

_____

_____

_____

_____

_____

What are 3 key responsibilities do you believe are important as a parent?

1._____

_____

2._____

_____

3._____

_____

MY LIFE JOURNAL

Use this page to share some more parenting stories or information and a family photo below

_____

_____

_____

_____

_____

_____

SECTION FIVE
LIFE, TRAVEL AND ADVENTURE

MY LIFE JOURNAL

If I could travel anywhere in the world for a holiday, I would visit..

_____

I would choose this location because..

_____

_____

_____

_____

_____

The activity or hobby that I enjoy most to participate now in is..

_____

_____

You could call it my 'super-power', but I have the unique ability to be able to....

_____

_____

_____

_____

MY LIFE JOURNAL

My biggest fear is....

_____

_____

_____

If I could invite 3 famous people to dinner (deceased or alive), they would be...

1. _____

2. _____

3. _____

If you could re-live and experience a personal moment in your life again, it would be?

_____

_____

_____

_____

_____

_____

_____

MY LIFE JOURNAL

Not many people would know this about me, so let me share it with you.

_____

_____

_____

_____

_____

_____

_____

If I could re-live and experience a moment in history (a world event), it would be..

_____

_____

_____

_____

_____

_____

My favourite quote of all time is.

I would recommend that everyone should read…

_____

One day in the future, I would like to be best remembered for…

_____

_____

_____

_____

_____

_____

_____

_____

MY LIFE JOURNAL

In no particular order, these are some of my proudest moments.

_____

_____

_____

_____

_____

_____

_____

_____

_____

_____

_____

_____

_____

_____

_____

_____

_____

MY LIFE JOURNAL

From my 20's, these are some of the jobs that I've had.
(Include the years if they can be recalled)

YEAR   EMPLOYMENT

_____   _____

_____   _____

_____   _____

_____   _____

_____   _____

_____   _____

_____   _____

_____   _____

_____   _____

_____   _____

_____   _____

_____   _____

_____   _____

_____   _____

MY LIFE JOURNAL

If I could have done anything as a job, it would have been..

_____

_____

The most interesting place I have ever visited has been..

_____

_____

_____

_____

_____

_____

_____

_____

_____

_____

_____ EXPLORE

MY LIFE JOURNAL

I feel the best way I can help others is by..

_____

_____

_____

_____

If someone was to write a book about my life, the title of the book would be..

_____

_____

I feel happiest when..

_____

_____

_____

_____

_____

_____

MY LIFE JOURNAL

If I had to choose another country to live in, it would be...

_____

because...

_____

_____

_____

These are 3 things that I would like to do over the next 12 months.

_____

_____

_____

_____

_____

_____

_____

_____

MY LIFE JOURNAL

Add any additional notes or information here..

_____

_____

_____

_____

_____

_____

_____

_____

_____

_____

_____

_____

_____

_____

_____

_____

SECTION SIX
MEMORIES AND STORIES

MY LIFE JOURNAL

The best family holiday I've experienced has been..

_____

_____

_____

_____

_____

_____

_____

_____

One of the hardest life experiences I've had to deal with was...

_____

_____

_____

_____

_____

MY LIFE JOURNAL

A great roadtrip I once experienced was...

_____

_____

_____

_____

_____

_____

_____

I had the best meal here and I will never forget it. In fact, I would highly recommend it!

_____

_____

_____

_____

_____

_____

—SECTION SEVEN—
MY FINAL WORDS

MY LIFE JOURNAL

Please include any further information, stories or moments that have not been shared throughout this journal.

MY LIFE JOURNAL

Please include additional photos, letters, postcards, certificates or other memorabilia in the pages provided.

ABOUT THE PUBLISHER

The Life Graduate Publishing Group was first established in 2019 with the key focus of creating high-quality books and resources to benefit customers worldwide.

With over 250 titles ranging from self-help books, children's books, journals, diaries, educational resources and sporting resources, The Life Graduate Publishing Group can now distribute books to a global customer audience using the world's largest Print on Demand (POD) services.

Please visit our website to view a range of our books and resources.

www.thelifegraduate.com/bookstore

A LIFETIME OF LEARNING.

Romney Nelson
Founder - The Life Graduate Publishing Group
International Best-Selling Author

OTHER GIFT BOOKS IN THE SERIES

Available for purchase via
www.thelifegraduate.com/bookstore
or major online bookstores

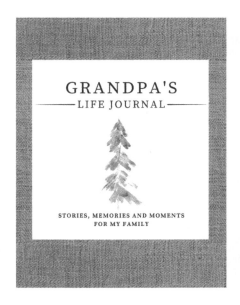

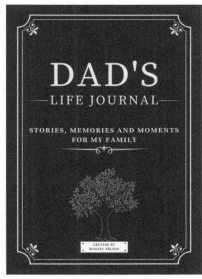

CPSIA information can be obtained
at www.ICGtesting.com
Printed in the USA
LVHW070526120523
746757LV00008B/631